BEHIND
NORMALCY

BEHIND NORMALCY

Burgi Zenhaeusern

Winner of the Harriss Poetry Prize
Kwame Alexander, Prize Series Editor
Erica Dawson, 2019 Prize Judge

CITYLIT
PRESS

Baltimore, Maryland

Library of Congress Control Number: 2019955758
ISBN 978-1-936328-24-6
CityLit Project is a 501(c)(3)
Nonprofit Organization
Federal Tax ID Number: 20-0639118
Printed in the United States of America
First Edition

2019 Prize Judge: Erica Dawson
www.ericadawsonpoet.net
Cover Photograph: Alan Sirulnikoff
www.sirulnikoff.ca
Author Photograph: Jorge Wong-Valle
Book Design: Gregg Wilhelm
Display Type: D-DIN Expanded Regular
Body Type: Plantagenet Cherokee

CITYLIT
PRESS

c/o CityLit Project
120 W. North Avenue
Baltimore, MD 21201
410.274.5691
www.CityLitProject.org
info@citylitproject.org

To you, reader.
You are a poem's lungs.

Contents

BEHIND
NORMALCY

Stirring Polenta

Hand-knit the socks of my childhood, sheep's
sallow beige, rough and itchy—no give in them.
Their fatty wool worked by our grandma
from a hard thread spun by her sister-in-law
      scratching the fingers of both.

Each summer, leaving behind hearty stews—
grandma's dug up potatoes and onions,
our collected blueberries mixed into
canned fruit—and her gorgeous bouquets
of endangered flowers she picked regardless,
we paid our great-uncle's house a visit,
stepped into the instantly blinding
dimness of a low-ceilinged dining room,
ground old dust into unhewn boards,
      knots pressing into our soles.

Our great-aunt in her dark layers ensconced
beside the cool soapstone of an idle oven.
There must have been an exchange of words,
shaking of hands, some more words
between dad and his uncle, brief laughs at
one of dad's jokes in the filtered afternoon
sun, pallid through small and deep-set windows,
      never a patch of it crossing her face.

If she smiled we wouldn't know nor how
many a sharp retort her expert fingers spun
into useful yarn, yarn for socks and gloves
for all of us—protection not comfort.
Soft treading from her corner always,
      her wheel a steady whir.

I still puzzle over the source of her light
in what I remember to be a pitch-dark
aisle of a kitchen, window slit at its end,
cast-iron stove, sink of stone, and a crate
filled with potatoes or cones to start
a fire—she must have known
       in her body each protrusion—

while slowly stirring a thickening
polenta, bubbles lazily
       mouthing along the surface.

I Can't Translate My Origins

Sliver of slate at best bouncing across
shimmer toward a bleeding

horizon, haze without
distance closing in.

I keep leaving from where
I left without arriving.

The shimmer keeps beckoning,
and so does the slim rock I weigh

between forefingers and thumb. I stand
sideways, shift my weight, and

concentric circles mark its path, and where
it sinks. Then silence.

aubade/s

behind
      the birds' swollen clamor
                           the beltway's
                           distant hum

normalcy
      reborn   (the feeling of)

      a draft from the cracked   window

            my first breath
            (fresh)

                  oblivion

                  then morning
      routine
            blinds drawn on what is

                  turning into

a dark June day
      leaves crawling with dim

            glimmer from the latest downpour

            and weeds—

                  bright green
fattening

music box

　　　　　　my pin-plucked off-beat
melody in your small hands
　　　　blue canopy
　　　　　　　gold-rimmed cresting

　　　　　　　　you stroke
　　　the smooth of my white plastic
miniature horses on golden rods
　　　　　　　　fetching
　　　me from the shelf and turn

the key to my sadness
　　　　　　　yet again
　　　what do you hear, little boy
　　　riding up and down
　　　round and round
I weep
　　　as you practice

breakfast on a school day

milk and butter bread and tea have to
get dressed breakfast's ready

      somebody lying on his back in a street strewn
      with litter flip flops people running in a panic

trying to shield his face is our picture
on the front page some Friday morning

      come now there's berries your favorite come
      his bare legs stretched out rigid in terror

next to the soldier's leveled muzzle about to spit
your vitamins take them finish eat

      flip-flops on the soldier's feet
      where are your socks go go it's late

snapped fractions before he fires
fact masked by the snapshot's caption

      decency   compassion   no time for that now
      brush your teeth it's late too late

for the photographer on his back all the time there is
no time I said get ready your book do you have

      your book I get it for you go ahead I'll catch up
      with that picture later

The Safety of Fear

I would my breath flickered *your*
pain, or what I deem to be yours, and *grief.*

Shuddering through the first few strokes—*a*
morning swim—I slowly sync with the *black-*

tiled line of the slain, my guide on the *ice-*
blue, leaf-strewn floor, a hair weaving through my fingers. *How*

chlorine burns contagion like silence into words. *I*
swim in a swirl of neutralized secretions—purity a *wish-*

ful thought—softly splashing *for*
fear packed like old *snow.*

Great Blue Heron

For many years I've kept a postcard
of the bird alighting on a rippled surface,
wings a royal spread, curved neck,
beak a graceful dagger, slender legs,
as bookmark, prayer at times, a yearning
for freedom, or harmony, or both, until I saw

a Great Blue Heron below the roar of Great Falls
land on a rock with a solemn flap,
saw it tense, then pierce the swirling fury
in one deft plunge, throw back its head, and lift
the rapier mandibles with their twitching prey—
lunge after lunge against an ever urging need.

to a deer in Rock Creek Park

did you know

how to wait

just long enough

this time for me

to pass you

on my lonely

stretch between

goal and goal, or was it

your whim, or a vague

sense of danger

that let you hesitate

there on the side

of the road like

dusk gathering shape

Tête-à-Tête with Mirror

Kindly contained
in soft weaves, you still

       full of life, mine
       and yours, pulsing out of reach.

I'm spread through you, tried
by your grip, searching

       you, thinking
       you couldn't make me

dread slowing rebirths,
thinking I

       didn't care
       so much about you

anyway, that I was
different—

self-portrait as *Granatöpfel*

                                from
                           yard
                    gnarled trees

                she taught us   to gather worm-
         fallobscht
littering the grass in
September humming
                with wasps   for *schnitz*
                             sometimes *muess*
                               or schnapps

not speckled skin
crayons wouldn't
          match but
    a fruit with
asymmetric halves
packed chambers
                one   wrong
                         squeeze
          red burst
splatter
              apply   gentle
                     pressure
      & the seeds   will
                       break
                   apart & sink

          blond

                   pith will float
                    tartness escapes
                         tongue

not
apples in my blood
my parents'

older than
mom
tunneled

not the pale
flesh protecting
the five-chambered
core that sticks
between your teeth
& cuts your gums

a fruit

bulged
globes
I   one in each palm
learned
to weigh   for juice
to score
a cradling   then break   open
underwater

learned   from a   leaflet
supermarket

to roof
pressed
sweet   tongue

[mottled shimmer the remnant]

mottled shimmer the remnant
of a shower in early March
quivering on the flagstones

a dusting of orange
on roughened rinds

the cobwebbing above
our street gleams

and turns
gray again

stiffness still between shoulder blades
while moisture has begun
to seep into the tight-fisted crust

mango

in your tongue / and

not the *chirsi* / of my home / *cerezas* in /

those twins & triplets / black pearls weather-split /

the stone propelled /

of your *patio's* bitter *limones* // your mom squeezed /

so

our separate paths / meandering alongside / away /

our child suckling his first right down to the pit /
to his fat belly in his aunt's arms on the beach /

skin spirals through my peeler / flesh slips / through

dark hours /

bites into the uncertain / firm

mango / on your tongue

slivers

in mine //

your dictionary // I picked /

twirled the supple / stems between my lips //

a wide arc // what do you know // what / do I /

a glass for me every morning //

much we can never be sure about // we harvest /

toward // do you remember /

juice dripping / from his pointy chin on
the fruit / as big as his face?

my fingers / morning gold / at these / still /

long before our hopeful

ness of *duraznos* / *pfirsich* / peaches //

and mine / soft /

expressed

portrait of my grandma as a young woman :: trees in February

my grandpa's lines	the hem they make
in ink so tremulous	against the cold
it's hard to believe	
my grandma was young	evening's turquoise
in that portrait	
hard to believe	antennae in the bluster
they came from the hand	
of the forceful strokes	
I had known him for	
as if his nib	
obeyed a trembling	

caress

along her face and neck	
his thumb gently rubbing	such filigreed
softness into the silk	assurance
of her collar	
obeyed his	now slowly disappearing
breathing	beyond the porchlight

At the Bus Stop

I'm following an airplane through sunlit
clouds at someone's gentle slope,
intense green below wan leaves

of late summer trees. I'm pilfering anything,
ready to wrap up at the sound of the bus
sure to hold my child and his needs.

For now, though, I'm light
forced through split clouds, and an on-and-off
glint silently cruising along.

Mountain Lake

Midday sun on unbroken
sheen. We all
went in toes first, or in one
reckless plunge
dared the cold. It sheathed
our flailing warmth, thrust us
up to gasp, shriek, or groan,
engulfed in its bursting.

        Afterwards, we laughed,
        sprawled on the warmed
        rise, the afternoon
        ahead of us. Un-rippling,
        the lake unveiled the felled
        trunks on pale ground.
        A pair of ducks, their quiet
                wakes mingling.

border/s

I say I can't translate
my origins
to say I belong

but I get to pilfer
from generous helpings
at the buffet's spread

I navigate
wounds
of this country

patience and curiosity
the only real border
I face

slowly un-
learning
'you'

safe I mean
from the threat of
being perceived as one

Boy on Backseat, Watching

In Managua
Why is this boy staring so at me? I don't know him.
What does he want, why is he there? Why isn't he
with the other kids skipping from car to car?
They hold things
close to the windows tapping the glass,
he just stares. I'm glad my window is up, though it's hot.
His feet are dirty, his clothes too, why
is he barefoot? I want him to go.

In Rockville
The boy in the car almost next to me,
what does he hold? Finally, he has seen me!
Oh, it's that nerf gun! Don't turn away!
Show me again! Oh no, we're moving
apart. We're still close enough!
I wanted to see if it is the one my friend has.

hidden in a grid of equal squares

among close-ups

of primary-

colored frogs

iridescent

birds and leaves

long lobed

and petals vividly

stained curled

pistils the size of

their faces

a boy and a girl

flora

and fauna of

some

endangered rainforest

two smiles in paradise

I'm made

to understand by this

checkered

print of it

on a bookmark

Leftovers:

Raw material for

New beginnings by rot

Absorbed by the yard's soft parts or someone else's

Splinters of bone or a fragile skull

I expected to find

The downs I did—snow white
        because the plucking, methodical and fierce,
        had to come first—

Here and there, but somewhere quite off

By the time I checked in spring

Of the Wood Duck that plummeted out of the sky into our yard
        in the talons of her predator, as big as the juvenile
        raptor herself (impossible to make off with it)

From the subsequent meal
        while we went from breakfast to lunch

That winter morning

Remains

Of a gift and its giver:

William Cooper, zoologist, collector of specimens, to
his friend, Charles Lucien Bonaparte, ornithologist,
ca. 1828; and hence

In a name: Accipiter cooperii
    (otherwise: Big Blue Darter, Chicken Hawk, Striker;
    Swift and Black-Capped)

Home Décor(um)

The portrait in the laundry room to its well-meaning owner:

You probably think 'us' beautiful
to have purchased her. Still, you could have

                                        placed her
                              above your mantel—
                    the rich folds of her white robe
              slipping from her glistening shoulders,
                  eyes smoldering under the loosely
                        wound headdress—ruling
                        your carefully positioned
            sofa, chair, and divan, the wide view
                on your luscious paradise.
Still,

                        you put her into the tight space
                              above your stainless
              washer/dryer combo—ebony skin and stare,
                    rag around her hair, shift a bunched
slippage—bursting your closet.

At a Red Light

I am one of those flimsy
plastic bags you get at checkout:

>rid of someone's stuff, a rustling
>skin dancing its trapped

pocket of air, a blown-out
mind atremble. Yes, follow

>my zigzagging lightness of being,
>and yes, believe I am breathing, forever

unfettered. I long to breach
your dammed lungs, unfurl

>in your sighs. Unless I get caught
>in the fork of a limb to whip the air

I will choke something
along the creek—feigning a film

>of dead leaves—where busy
>hands may collect me, the rotten

treasure that I am, in garbage bags: plastic
to plastic. You're still gazing.

[after days of sun gray]

after days of sun gray
feels unreal
all day like dusk

an apple on
the pile shifts slightly
and up the street a hammer
goes from head to head
the same few
measures on wood

erratic spurts through dry leaves
of squirrels chasing
after each other

pushed clouds

sometimes you don't
see what is
rearing up to speak
from you
until you say it
recognition always
too late

the apple a bite
into mealiness
and the hammer
            the hammer

Catch

Breached ears this morning
fighting to un-hear
news of human bombs, bullets: his first

tears for more than himself, tears
as slow to form as permanent teeth.
I'm bound to watch

                        his wounded
righteousness—wonderful
catch in my web of gutted carcasses.

Greed

Flicker of her naked
feet (someone else's zooming)
pulled close:

> Her socks among the frozen
> wash outside, I guess.
> Her missing
> shoes—she must have
> fled in some—
> drying from the snow, I hope.
> And whose
> shoes are burning
> in that metal box, a charred
> pot on top steaming?

A girl (zoomed out), huddled
in the half-dark of boards barely
joined to walls, a roof
against no weather, a girl
quite possibly no longer
there.

> My need to be
> forgiven is all
> I know.

Mass at Easter in the Alps

Unadorned the walls,
and unadorned the voices

that evenly pour into
the space between me and up

on high. I am cold
like last night's fire,

and the sitting is hard
in the age-old pew. My child

has started to grasp some facts. Christ—
greenish yellow with dark red

gashes—on a crucifix. The Body.
Offered up. Piles of bodies

on pictures in school:
What can I learn from piles

but to look away! he asks.
And the voices rise

and fall, swell and fade
stilling on the tip of the tongue.

He pulls, pulls me away
from the bench, the voices that sound

notes the length of my breath, clear as bells'
remote tolling, all the way to his climb,

where up high he is aiming, and where I'll try
to have his back as I used to.

Rubber Glove

Soft armor, slough of
the firm touch. I've shed
mine, pink, medium size, limp

shell of a grip out there,

translucent skin instead,
moist and shivering
in the alien sun. I pray.

Notes

"breakfast on a school day"
  The Japanese Photographer, Kenji Nagai, died of multiple gunshot wounds in late September of 2007 covering protests in Burma (*Washington Post*, September 28, 2007).

"The Safety of Fear"
  The line used in this acrostic poem is from "Work Calendar " from *Haint: poems* © 2016 by Teri Ellen Cross Davis, used by permission of Gival Press.

"Rubber Glove"
  Based on the image "Pink Glove on Sidewalk" by photographer Alan Sirulnikoff.

Acknowledgments

I am grateful to the editors of the following journals for publishing my poems:

Passager: "I Can't Translate My Origins"

Forage Poetry: "Great Blue Heron"

UCity Review: "to a deer in Rock Creek Park," "[mottled shimmer the remnant]," "Leftovers," and "[after days of sun gray]"

Diagram: "self-portrait as *Granatöpfel*"

American Poetry Journal: "portrait of grandma as a young woman :: trees in February"

Oversound: "hidden in a grid of equal squares"

Gargoyle: "Mass at Easter in the Alps"

Heron Tree: "Rubber Glove"

My deep gratitude goes to Erica Dawson and Kwame Alexander for serving as 2019 judge and series editor, respectively, and for giving my manuscript their support; to my editor Gregg Wilhelm for making it all happen, including the many formatting challenges; to Executive Director Carla du Pree and everyone at CityLit Project for providing the opportunity of the Harriss Poetry Prize; to poets Teri Ellen Cross Davis and Molly Spencer for their kind and generous words; to my photographer friend Alan

Sirulnikoff for letting me use his image, and to my poet friend Susan Okie for lending this manuscript her eyes and ears; and, most of all, to everybody for sharing their time with it. Thank you to my friends and family for their unflagging encouragement. To Jorge and Adrian always.

Praise for *Behind Normalcy*

"*Behind Normalcy* is an opportunity to explore the tense and probing questions we hide behind and hide from in polite society. From the juxtaposition of sending a child off to school as a photographer's death makes front page news, to the great aunt the poet knows best by her handmade socks, Burgi Zenhaeusern has the patience and the eye to peel back the layers of everyday and reveal the small truths lying beneath. In [after days of sun gray] she writes,

> sometimes you don't
> see what is
> rearing up to speak
> from you
> until you say it

I am glad she is saying it. In succinct, pure lines, she documents the quiet beauty of this fragmented and complex world."

— Teri Ellen Cross Davis
Author of *Haint*
Poetry Coordinator
Folger Shakespeare Library

"'I'm pilfering anything,' confesses the speaker in Burgi Zenhaeusern's *Behind Normalcy*, and it's true. These poems shimmer with the commonplace—an apple shifting in the bowl, a rubber glove, the bus stop, a plastic shopping bag blown in the wind, our endless wars. In these pages are ordinary moments made to gleam by the poet's clean attention, formal daring, and quietly startling images. Moments made to gleam by the poet's zigzag through the day, through memory and the natural world, through the 'blinding dimness,' to remind us that the ordinary is only ordinary if we don't look closely. Come to these poems and let them soothe the blur of days. Let them show you where and why and how 'the shimmer keeps beckoning.'"

— Molly Spencer
Author of *If the House*
Professor, Gerald R. Ford School of Public Policy
University of Michigan

"With a keen eye for detail and deft use of form, Zenhaeusern writes lovely narratives and lyrics drawing our attention to the urgency of both grief and hope. This is a wonderful collection."

— Erica Dawson
Author of *When Rap Spoke Straight to God*
Director, MFA in Creative Writing
University of Tampa

About the Poet

Burgi Zenhaeusern, originally from Switzerland, lives with her husband in Chevy Chase, Maryland, where she is involved in the literary community as the publicity volunteer for a local reading series. Her writing appears in several print and online journals. burgizenhaeusern.com.

About CityLit Press

CityLit Press's mission is to provide a venue for writers who might otherwise be overlooked by larger publishers due to the literary nature or regional focus of their projects. It is the imprint of nonprofit CityLit Project, founded in Baltimore in 2004.

CityLit nurtures the culture of literature in Baltimore and throughout Maryland by creating enthusiasm for literature, building a community of avid readers and writers. Thank you to our major supporters: the National Endowment for the Arts, the Maryland State Arts Council, the Baltimore Office of Promotion and The Arts, and the Robert W. Deutsch Foundation. More information and documentation is available at www.guidestar.org.

Additional support is provided by individual contributors. Financial support is vital for sustaining the ongoing work of the organization. Secure on-line donations can by made at our web site (click on "Donate"). Thank you!

CityLit is a member of the Greater Baltimore Cultural Alliance, the Maryland Association of Nonprofit Organizations, Maryland Citizens for the Arts, and the Writers' Conferences and Centers division of the Association of Writing Programs (AWP).

For information about CityLit Press and public programs offered by CityLit Project, please visit www.citylitproject.org.

About the Harriss Poetry Prize

Launched in 2009 under the guidance of poet and former CityLit Project chair Michael Salcman, the Harriss Poetry Prize is named in honor of Clarinda Harriss, eminent Baltimore poet, publisher, and professor of English at Towson University. Harriss, educated at Johns Hopkins University and Goucher College, is a widely published, award-winning poet and she serves as director of BrickHouse Books, Maryland's oldest literary press, which *Baltimore* magazine named "Best of Baltimore."

2019 Judge: Erica Dawson
2014 Judge: Michael Salcman
2013 Judge: Marie Howe
2012 Judge: Tom Lux
2011 Judge: Dick Allen
2010 Judge: Michael Salcman

Today, the prize is awarded every other year. For complete guidelines, please go to www.citylitproject.org and click on "CityLit Press." Send entry fee, manuscript with table of contents, acknowledgments, and two coversheets (one with name, title, mailing address, daytime phone, and email address and one with title only) to:

Harriss Poetry Prize
CityLit Press
c/o CityLit Project
120 W. North Avenue
Baltimore, MD 21201
www.citylitproject.org

Harriss Poetry Prize Winners

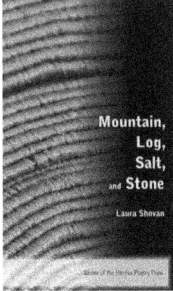

Mountain, Log, Salt, and Stone
by Laura Shovan ISBN: 978-1936328-02-4
"Laura Shovan enlivens her quotidian
subjects with a shrewd and powerful use of
metaphor, a critical strategy all too often
neglected in contemporary work."
Michael Salcman, Judge

Famous by Bruce Sager
ISBN: 978-1936328-06-2
"Only twice before, in the many times I've
judged poetry contests, has a poet's work
stood out as strongly as Sager's."
Dick Allen, Judge

Every Bit of It by Katherine Bogden
ISBN: 978-1936328-08-6
"This book reveals by what it hides. It tells
a deeply human story and tells it slant, as
Emily Dickinson said, when, I believe, she
was talking about how originality might
come about. And that's what these poems
are: original. And alive."
Tom Lux, Judge

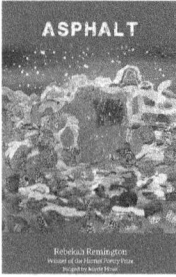

Asphalt by Rebekah Remington
ISBN: 978-1936328-15-4
"I love how Remington's mind moves from this to that in some utterly lived syllogism ('What looks like failure is something else'). I love how the poet—desperate as the rest of us—loves the world."

Marie Howe, Judge

Oblige the Light by Danuta Kosk-Kosicka
ISBN: 978-1936328-15-4
"A magical space—astonishing metaphors and precise description of natural forces and historical events result in an atmospheric Magical Realism that borders on the Surrealistic."

Michael Salcman, Judge

Other Poetry Books from CityLit Press

An Easy Place / To Die
by Vincent A. Cellucci ISBN: 978-1936328-03-1
  "Cellucci's debut collection is a kind
of bricolage monument to New Orleans,
constructed with whatever is at hand: images,
facts, mini-flights of rhetoric, and snippets of
overheard speech are all juxtaposed."

James Capozzi
noladiaspora.org

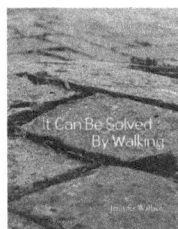

It Can Be Solved By Walking
by Jennifer Wallace ISBN: 978-1936328-05-5
  "A passionate attachment to the heartbeat
of language shapes these meditations by
which Wallace sifts Baltimore's grief and
beauty for gold."

Lia Purpura

Lo-fi Poetry Series
Poets Cover Your Record Collection

Clash by Night
LaFemina and Wilhelm, Eds.
ISBN: 978-1936328-17-8

Poets Sounds
LaFemina and Stroud, Eds.
ISBN: 978-1936328-21-5